THIS BOOK OF PROMISES IS GIVEN TO:

_____

AS A GIFT FROM:

_____

DATE AND OCCASION:

_____

*"Do not seek Me for what I can do,
but for who I Am," saith the Lord.*

# Promises

## GOD'S PROVISION THROUGH HIS PROMISES

### SHEILA KAY

MANIFEST
PUBLICATIONS

# DEDICATION

I dedicate this book to my Great-Grand Daughter

**Danielle Elizabeth Headley**

That she may know her greatest friend in this life and beyond, who is, and will always be, the great I AM:

**Almighty God – Father – Son – Holy Spirit**

Your name Daniel means, *God is judge*

Your name Elizabeth means, *God is my oath*

*God is saying to you today, Danielle:* "For I love you greatly, and will be with you always. Be still, know that I am your God, and I hear your every word and thought. Call on me when you are in need or just to tell me how much you love me," saith the Lord. Danielle, your Great Nana Kay hears from God, talks with God, and walks with God. You too can have this privilege…

## A Word of Prophecy for each of my Grandchildren:

**John**: '*God is gracious.*' "And you shall preach the word of Almighty God, you shall be called a Prophet/Preacher," saith the Lord.

**Joseph**: '*Dreamer and interpreter of dreams, a seer.*' "Take your eyes off the world and turn them to Me," saith the Lord," for I love you like none other could. You do not know the plans I have for you but seek me first and I will show you things you know not of."

**Thomas**: '*The twin.*' "Do not seek assurance or reassurance from others, but from Me. Ask, and it shall be given; seek, and it shall be found; knock, and your door will open, for your destiny lies with Me," saith the Lord. "You are my chosen!" saith the Lord.

**Jessie**: '*Wealthy.*' "May the God of hope fill you with all joy and peace in believing, that ye may abound in hope through the power of the Holy Spirit," saith the Lord.

# TABLE OF CONTENTS

# FOREWORD
### By: Prophet David Harmon

## 'God Has Given His Word'

When someone has given their word concerning a matter, they vow a claim that puts the integrity of their character at stake, and produces expectancy in that, what has been spoken with assurance will, in fact, be performed in truth.

When they actually do as they have told us, we look again to that same person to maintain the integrity and character by acting upon and accomplishing the further guarantee of their words toward us.

Such a person we rely on until we consider them trustworthy; so, their word is good, and their promise can be believed; someone with whom which we could wish to make ourselves vulnerable and call friend!

This is the core of who we are in the real meeting between personhood and personhood, which touches upon the deepest sense of what we desire as relationship!

Yet when the words of men and women fail us, as, sooner or later they are bound to do, and relationships come short of all the things we have anticipated; and even when we disappoint ourselves by our own inadequacies, where then do we turn? Where is the acting out of truth we are looking for?

Who then do we trust?

# INTRODUCTION

And He spoke to me saying:
**"Gather my words of promise as a mother gathers her chicks! Tenderly and lovingly."**

I have prayed over the Word of Almighty God in selecting what He would have me put before you on these pages. Not of meat, drink, and outward religion but of Righteousness, Peace, Joy, and Direction.

Words and Promises, found in the Book of Romans, that can help lead the lost to the cross.

Words and Promises found throughout the New Testament, which when spoken or prayed, can bring healing to our body, or the body of others.

Words of hope that dry tears and give comfort to those who mourn or feel so all alone.

Words of direction, leading us in the way the Lord would have us go, as we live our life by the Word.

Words conveying the forgiveness of sins and the greatness of our God.

Words that assure us of unlimited power; that the power Christ has we have also, giving us the ability to lay hands on the sick and know they shall recover.

These words give us an answer to prayer according to faith. But also, punishment in hell and decrees of punishment for rebels!

The writing of this small book has filled me afresh with the wonderful and powerful word of Almighty God. Healing has fallen upon me, and new revelation has come forward. I thank You Lord and give you praise for the divine assurance you have given us through your Promises!

There are 750 promises in the New Testament, in 250 different categories. There are many such treasures hidden throughout the Bible. The words on the following pages are given as Promises that we may claim daily. Carry this book with you, claim HIS promises for your life and over the lives of your family, friends and the lost you encounter daily.

Each of us has been chosen! We are that vessel, that conduit He uses to reach the lost. We have a mighty responsibility, let us not be sluggards, but mighty in our calling. Be blessed, be strong and be bold, with the boldness of Almighty God.

*For He is the Bread of Life, just take and eat,*
*Life is in HIS Words.*

*He is a rewarder of them that diligently seek Him.*
*Hebrews11:6b*

We are only touching the surface within these pages, but each word is given by God.

*Jesus said, "Man shall not live by bread alone, but, by every Word that proceeds out of the mouth of God!" (Matthew 4:4.)*

That, my friend, is a promise, spoken to you, by Jesus! *"Don't seek me for what I can do, but for who I AM,"* saith the Lord. And, "I will never leave thee, nor forsake thee." (Hebrews 13:5.)

*There is miracle-working Power in HIS Word!*

*I encourage you to bring the promises within these pages to His remembrance.*

**These promises are for YOU!**

# *One*

## PROVISION THROUGH PROMISES

God's provisions are made available to us through His promises. These promises are found in His Word, the Holy Bible. The only excuse for not having every need and want met within the bounds of Scripture is *unbelief and ignorance of truth.* (See Matthew 17:20-21; James 1:5-8; Hebrews 11:6.) The doctrine of "no want" to believers is one of the clearest and most comprehensive declarations of Scripture. God will not withhold anything good from us, according to His Word, providing that we meet *three conditions laid out for us*: 1. Fear the Lord; 2. Seek the Lord; 3. Walk Up-rightly. The promises are simple, complete and easy to understand.

1. We must fear the Lord.

Psalms 34:9 O fear the LORD, ye His saints: for there is *no want to them that fear Him.*

Proverbs 8:13 The **fear** of the LORD is to: *hate evil, pride, arrogance, and the evil way, and a froward* *[perverse; deceitful] mouth.*

The Hebrew word for *fear* in the term "fear of the Lord" is *yir'ah, concordance reference number H3374 (fear, reverence, awe, piety)* If one truly recognizes God as all-powerful, this will be reflected in his attitude and daily life in the form of reverence.

2. We Must Seek the Lord.

Psalms 34:10 The young lions do lack, and suffer hunger: *but they that* **seek** *the LORD* shall not want for any good thing.

We must seek the Lord:
    a.  With all your heart (Deuteronomy 4:29.)
    b.  Continually (1 Chronicles 16:11.)
    c.  By humbling self (2 Chronicles 7:14.)
    d.  By prayer (without ceasing.)
    e.  By turning from sin (daily.)
    f.  By preparing the heart (2 Chronicles 19:3.)
    g.  Diligently seek Him (Hebrews 11:6.)

*Hosea 10:12 ...for it is time to* **seek the Lord** *until He comes and rains righteousness upon you (the seeker.)*

The Hebrew word for *seek* is *baqash. (Concordance reference number H1245)* It means: *seek, search, consult.* Scripture also promises that when we seek God, we will find Him, He will answer us, and even reward us. He will be found (1 Chronicles 28:9), He will hear and answer (2 Chronicles 7:14), we will not want for anything (Psalm.34:9-10). *He is a rewarder of them that diligently seek Him* (Hebrews 11:6.)

3. We Must Walk Uprightly.

Psalms 84:11 For the LORD God is a sun and shield: the LORD will give grace and glory: no good thing will be withheld from *them that walk uprightly.*

To walk uprightly is to:
  a.  Walk in the way of God's judgment (Isaiah 26:8.)
  b.  Wait for the LORD to lead.
  c.  Desire the name of God.
  d.  Remember the LORD.
  e.  Desire God with your whole heart and soul (Isaiah 26:9.)
  f.  Seek God early with your spirit.
  g.  Learn righteousness through the chastening of God (Hebrews 12:5-13.)

The Hebrew word for *uprightly* is *tamim. (Concordance number H8549.)* It is the divine standard which man must attain. To walk upright in one's conduct, faultless, innocent, blameless (literally, morally and figuratively) whole.

By our eternal right through Jesus Christ the following

7

are given to His people, and they belong to His followers as they did King David. Power, riches, wisdom, strength, honor, glory and blessings (1 Chronicles. 29:12 and Deuteronomy 8:18) are all in the LORD'S Hand and He is able to make great and to give strength to all.

## PUTTING OUR FAITH IN THE CROSS

Once we put our faith in Christ's atoning death, on our behalf, we become legal heirs of God and joint-heirs with Christ (Romans 8:17.) Jesus took all the evil we deserve so that we might receive all the good He deserves. We are called now to trust in the exchange of grace. Jesus was wounded that we might be healed (Isaiah 53:4-5.) He was made to be sin with our sinfulness so *that we might be made righteous with His righteousness.* (2 Corinthians 5:21.) He was rejected by the Father *that we might be accepted by the Father* (Matthew 27:46; Ephesians 1:5-6.) He died our death that *we might have His life.* (Hebrews 2:9.)

Through our faith in what Jesus did for us, we become members of God's family and *entitled to all that was promised to Abraham.* (Galatians 3:7-9, 29.) "In thee shall all nations be blessed." This is called the gospel or glad tidings for all nations. All who are partakers of this must likewise be justified by faith. We now live by grace through faith! (Galatians 3:11b.) "For, the just [good character, holy, innocent] shall live by faith."

We now have a relationship with the Triune God, our Father, Son, Holy Spirit! (John 17:3.) "And this is life eternal; that they might know thee, the only true God."

## THE NAMES OF GOD

There is only one God who is the Creator of the Universe. This one God has revealed Himself in His Word through various names which highlight the many aspects of who He is, His ability to follow through on His promises, and His willingness to do so.

**Elohim**: God, the Creator.
This is the first name of God in the Scriptures and is used to describe Him as the Creator of heaven and earth. (Genesis 1:1.) The name of God in Hebrew is El, and it describes God's power, creativity, glory, and tremendous majesty. Coupling El with *ohim* changes the word to be plural which is our first indication of the Trinity of the Godhead, including the Father, Son, and Holy Spirit. This is the power of God personified. In the beginning, God who is the divine power of the Father, Son, and Holy Spirit, created heaven and earth. Everything that was ever made was made by this Triune God in their unimaginable power.

**Jehovah**: the Lord my God.
This is an intimate, personal God and Lord. A present tense name of God for the *now*. This is the God of promise.

9

**El Shaddai**: God, my Supplier.

Again, El is the name for God indicating power and strength. Shaddai denotes abundance, the double-breasted one who nourishes. (Genesis 17:1-2.)

All of the Names of God play a remarkable part in releasing promises in us, to us and through us, as He reveals Himself to us through intimate, personal and loving situations. I have only addressed a few of His glorious names in detail to show the connection to His promises. Here are a few more of God's glorious names.

**Adonai**: Lord, my Master.

**Jehovah Jireh**: the Lord my Provider.

**Jehovah Rophe**: the Lord my Healer.

**Jehovah Nissi**: the Lord my Banner.

**Jehovah Mikkahesh**: the Lord my Sanctifier.

**Jehovah Tsidkenu**: the Lord my Righteousness.

**Jehovah Shalom**: the Lord my Peace.

**Jehovah Rohi**: the Lord my Shepherd.

**Jehovah Shammah**: the Lord who is Here (Your Abiding Presence is here.)

*Two*

# THE PROMISE OF THE HOLY SPIRIT

The key to all other blessings is *the promise of the Holy Spirit.* He alone can bring us into the *fullness of the Spirit* through faith in the cross and all that it encompasses. (See Matthew 3:11; Luke 24:29; John 7:37-39; Acts 1:4-8, 2:33, 38-39; Galatians 3:13.)

Just as *"the Lord had blessed Abraham in all things"* (Genesis 24:1) we became members of God's family and entitled to *all that was promised* Abraham (Galatians 3:7-9, 29) so that we may receive the blessing of Abraham *"in all things."* God is able to make *all* grace **abound** toward you; that ye, always having *all* sufficiency in *all* things, may **abound** to every good work (2 Corinthians 9:8.)

*Examine yourself!*
*To receive God's abundance towards us,*
*our motives and attitudes must be pleasing to God.*

During the past twenty years, I have worked in the prison systems in the capacity of food-service director,

11

working with male and female inmates while training and preparing them for re-entry into the workplace with usable job skills. While working in a classroom setting or one-on-one, it does not take long to realize they were abused as children. Often, they were never nurtured, held, cuddled, or loved the way a child should be. Today, that is called being from dysfunctional homes. But what is a functional home? Can't most homes be defined as dysfunctional?

Most of the inmates had horrendous stories of being violated on an ongoing basis, hiding under beds or in closets to avoid being found. I felt honored that they were comfortable confiding in me. It gave them release from acts they had buried so deep within themselves for so many years. It also gave me the opportunity to minister to them about forgiveness and often, to rid themselves from feelings of guilt.

Much hate and un-forgiveness is visible. Many blame themselves for what happened to them, and all are in need of the LORD. They have told of being raped as small children (many by the same sex); and ongoing abuse which was often done to them by a family member, a mother's boyfriend, a neighbor, baby-sitter, or by house guests or friends. Because of so much pent-up shame and guilt, many dropped out of school at an early age. There was never anyone to encourage them and no one to help with homework. Because of the environment, they continued to live in sin.

In truth, regardless of what we have experienced or what has been done to us, much of the mess our lives may be in presently could be the result of many of our own wrong or poor decisions. No matter the reason for our sin or condition, forgiveness of self and others is possible while we ask for God's forgiveness.

Our total surrender is needed. Give it all to God! Ask Him to take all thoughts from your mind. The generational curse is a real thing but does not have to be a reality in our lives. Call on Him; He is faithful to answer.

According to the Bible, God spoke to Jeremiah and said, "Before I formed you in the belly, I knew you; and before you came forth out of the womb I sanctified thee, and I ordained thee a prophet…." (Jeremiah 1:5.) God has had the plan for your life before you were born. I find this beautiful! We were spirits formed by God prior to entering our mother's womb.

We Are a
**SPIRIT**
*Either good or evil.*

We Have a
Soul
*We accept or reject sin.*

We Have a
Body
*Sin tries to enter.*

God gave each of us choices. If sin enters our body through the *eye gate* (what you look at with your eyes) or the *ear gate* (what you hear with your ears), or *any of your senses*, y*our soul* must reject or accept it. Entering through the eye gate could be pornography, movies with violent or sexual content, magazines, observed violent or sinful behavior, written sayings, books, brutality, etc. This includes listening to off-colored jokes, filthy language, distasteful music, gossip, garbage in, garbage out. Any or all of these could become addictions, obsessions and lead you down a path toward and through a sinful way of life.

### *If sin is fed, it grows!*

We were all dealt a different hand in life but in Hebrews 13:5, God said to us, "I will never leave thee nor forsake thee." *This is a promise.* Cry out to Him; He is waiting!

The Bible says, "Choose you today who you will serve." (Joshua 24:15.) The secret to making the right decisions is *always reject sin and choose to follow Christ.* Ask the Lord to clear these thoughts or actions from you. He will!

*Pray:*
*Lord Jesus, cleanse my mind,*
*cleanse my heart, cleanse my tongue*
*and guide me!*

We must be determined to be strong, learning to take authority over ourselves, in what we do and what we become, living a consecrated life deliberately through the Holy Spirit. All we have ever had to do is turn to

Him, for He is there. He will always be there, and from now until this body dies, as long as we have breath we can call out to Him and He will be there. (After the last breath it is too late!) We are covenant partners with the Lord, and there is a need for righteousness before God.

*God does not want to be a part of our life, for we are part of His life!* We are made in His image. He is not made in our image. *We are to be like Him.*

*Jesus promised us the gift of the Comforter. This promise, this gift, is the Holy Spirit.*

## WHO IS THE HOLY SPIRIT?

The Holy Spirit is the third person of the God Head and was there in the beginning. "And the earth was without form, and void; and darkness was upon the face of the deep. And *the Spirit of God* moved upon the face of the waters." (Genesis 1:2.)

Even in your life, when things are at their worst, as it was in, know that the Holy Spirit is moving, He is hovering over you. Cry out to God! *(Note: Do not pray or call out to the Holy Spirit, always to God in the name of Jesus.)*

The Holy Spirit is such a vast subject and we know so little about Him. Nevertheless, God in His Word has revealed all we need to know. The Holy Spirit is a

15

person, with personality, a nature, and He is God-an equal part of the three-person God-Head. He speaks (Acts 28:25); teaches (John 14:26); strives with sinners (Genesis 6:3); comforts (Acts 9:31); helps our infirmities (Romans 8:26); He is grieved (Ephesians 4:30); He is resisted (Acts 9:51); He is the Spirit of Jesus Christ (John 14:18; Galatians 4:6).

**The Holy Spirit is the mind of Christ: Let this mind be in you, which was also in Christ Jesus.**
*Philippians.2:5*

**We have the mind of Christ.**
*1 Corinthians 2:16*

The Holy Spirit is described as a "gift." (John 14:16-21, 26, 16:7-15; Ephesians 1:13-23; 1 Thessalonians 4:8.)

The Holy Spirit is a gift we can ask for. "How much more shall your heavenly Father give the Holy Spirit to them who ask Him." (Luke 11:13.)

### WHAT IS THE PURPOSE OF THE HOLY SPIRIT?

The Holy Spirit is given to believers that we may live a holy life, staying focused on the cross. "Be ye holy as I am Holy," saith the LORD. (1 Peter 1:16.) "Because ye are sons, God has sent forth the Spirit of His Son into your heart." (Matthew 26:28.)

The Angel of the LORD appeared to Joseph in a dream telling him to take Mary as his wife: "For that which is conceived in her is of the Holy Ghost. And she shall bring forth a Son, and thou shalt call His name JESUS; for *He shall save His people from their sin*." (Matthew 1:20-21.)

This is a promise. The name Jesus in Hebrew is Yehoshua which means *Jehovah Saves*. When Jesus spoke of a Lost Sheep in the parable in Luke 15:3-7 and Matthew 18:11, He said: "For the Son of man *is come to save that which was lost*." Moreover, in Matthew 26:28, Jesus spoke, "For this is my blood of the new testament, which is *shed for many for the remission of sins.*"

We experience the Holy Spirit in different personal ways, dependent on our faithfulness and obedience. *The Holy Spirit can work only to the level of our obedience.* He is the Helper, our Comforter, our Advocate with the Father, and our Parakletos (our intercessor) of whom Jesus said, "I will send unto you from the Father." (John 15:26.)

He is the Holy Ghost whom the Father sends in the name of Jesus to teach us all things and brings all things to our remembrance. (John 14:26.) He is the Spirit of the Father who speaks in us and through us. (Matthew10:20.) "For it is not you that speaks but the Spirit of your Father that speaks in you."

17

We are told, "Humble yourself as a little child" (Mark 9:33-37; Luke 9:46-48.) Matthew 18:5 says, "and *whosoever shall receive one such little child in my name receiveth Me.*"

Matthew 18:18 speaks of when one brother sins against another how we are to go to him. The Lord seeks harmony between us all. Jesus said, "Whatsoever ye shall *bind on earth shall be bound in heaven*: and whatsoever ye *shall loose on earth shall be loosed (destroy, dissolve, put off) in heaven."*

Humility is shown in Matthew 19:30 "But many that are first shall be last, and the last shall be first." Also in Matthew 20:28, Jesus said, "Even as the Son of man came not to be ministered unto, but to minister, *and to give His life a ransom for many."*

Matthew 5:2-12 is known as the Sermon on the Mount, dealing with the state of mind and heart of a true Christian disciple. Each beatitude tells us how to be blessed by God.

*Blessed is the poor in spirit; for **theirs is the kingdom of heaven**.*

*Blessed are they that mourn; **for they shall be comforted.***

*Blessed are the meek; for **they shall inherit the earth**.*

*Blessed are they who hunger and thirst after righteous: **for they shall be filled.***

*Blessed are the merciful: for they **shall obtain mercy**.*

*Blessed are the pure in heart; for **they shall see God**.*

*Blessed are the peacemakers; for **they shall be called the children of God**.*

*Blessed are they who are persecuted for righteousness sake: for **theirs is the kingdom of heaven**.*

***Blessed are you** when men shall revile and persecute and shall say all manner of evil against you falsely, for my sake.* Rejoice, and be exceeding glad: ***for great is your reward in heaven**:* for so persecuted they the prophets which were before you.

Matthew 5:19: He whosoever, therefore, shall break one of these commandments and shall teach men so, he **shall be called least** in the kingdom of heaven, but *whosoever shall do and teach them [commandments], the same **shall be called great in the kingdom of heaven**.*

Matthew 18:19: Again I say unto you, ***that if two of you shall agree*** on earth as touching anything that they shall ask, ***it shall be done for them*** of My Father which is in heaven.

Matthew 18:20: For where *two or three are gathered together in My name*, there ***am I in the midst [middle] of them.***

19

Two can move God for whatever they ask and agree upon in prayer, and when two or more gather, He is there!

Material Blessings are given as shown in Matthew 19:29: Jesus said, "And every one that hath forsaken houses, or brethren, or sisters, or father, or mother or wife, or children, or lands, for my name's sake, *shall receive a hundredfold, and shall inherit everlasting life."*

Matthew 24:35: Heaven and earth shall pass away, but *My Word shall not pass away.*

Matthew 26:29: But "I say unto you, I will not drink henceforth of this fruit of the vine, until that day *when I drink it new with you in My Father's kingdom*."
This is at the second advent, and into all eternity that Christ will partake of eating and drinking with all the resurrected saints. What a glorious day that will be!

## WHAT IS THE PROMISE OF THE HOLY SPIRIT?

During the preaching of John the Baptist, these words were conveyed to people while telling them about repentance and turning from their sin. "I indeed baptize you with water unto repentance." These words spoken by John were claimed in Matthew, Mark, and Luke.

These are confirmed promises.

a. But *He (Jesus) shall **baptize you with the Holy Ghost, and with fire.*** " The baptism is to "fulfill all righteousness," the Holy Ghost refers to the spiritual rebirth of the regeneration and the fire is the result of judgment [purging and burning of the chaff.] (Matthew. 3:11-12; Luke 3:16.)

b. John the Baptist speaking, "I have indeed baptized you with water; *but He [Jesus] shall **baptize you with the Holy Ghost.*** " (Mark 1:8.)

c. John the Baptist speaking: "And I knew Him not, but He that sent me to baptize with water, the same said unto me; 'Upon whom thou shalt see the Spirit descending, and the same is ***He which baptizes with the Holy Ghost.*** ' And I saw, and bare record that this is the Son of God." (John 1:33-34.)

When Jesus came, He confirmed what John preached. He stood and cried, saying, "If any man thirst, let him come unto Me and drink. He that believeth on Me, as scripture hath said, ***out of his belly shall flow rivers of living water.*** " (John 7:37-38.) He also told His disciples, "But ***ye shall receive power, after that the Holy Ghost is come upon you;*** and ye shall be witnesses unto me both in Jerusalem and in all Judea, and in Samaria and unto the uttermost part of the earth. (Acts 1:8.)

***These are promises!***

21

One of the characteristics of the future reign of Christ is the abundant outpouring of the Holy Spirit. On the day of Pentecost, Peter recognized that the outpouring anticipated an even greater outpouring yet to come.

*"And it shall come to pass in the last days,"* **saith God,** *"I will pour out of My Spirit upon all flesh; and your sons and daughters shall prophesy and your young men shall see visions and your old men shall dream dreams; and on My servants and on My handmaidens* **I will pour out in those days of my Spirit; and they shall prophesy.** *And* **I will show wonders in heaven above, and signs in the earth beneath;** *blood, and fire and vapor of smoke.* **The sun shall be turned into darkness and the moon into blood, before that great day of the LORD come.** *And it shall come to pass that* **whosoever shall call on the Name of the Lord shall be saved."** *(Acts 2:17-21.)*

Jesus speaking: "And, behold, I send *the promise of my Father* upon you: but tarry you in the city of Jerusalem, *until we be endued with power from on high."* (Luke 24:49.)

This power is the strength for Evangelism. The Spirit's coming was not an afterthought but an integral part of God's eternal will. In Matthew 4:19, Jesus speaks to His fishermen disciples, saying, *"Follow Me and I will make you fishers of men*." And they followed him. They became evangelists with soul-winning power.

Another promise given by Jesus is the victory over temptation. *"Man shall not live by bread alone, but by every word that proceeds out of the Mouth of God."* (Matthew 4:4; Luke 4:4.) Jesus said in John 4:32, "I have meat to eat that ye know not of." His source of strength was always *obedience to the Father's will. This obedience is our strength as well.*

In Matthew 6:30, Jesus teaches that God is not only our creator but also promises to be our sustainer. "Wherefore, if God so clothe the grass of the field, which today is, and tomorrow is cast into the oven, *shall He not much more clothe you*, O ye of little faith?"

Matthew 7:7: *Ask, and it shall be given you; seek, and you shall find; knock, and it shall be opened unto you.* The three imperatives, Ask, Seek and Knock are in the present tense. It is for today, as it was then, and refers to the answer of our prayers. We can trust and know that God will answer because of His love for us as our heavenly Father. Matthew 7:11 says, "If you then, being evil, know how to give good gifts unto your children, *how much more shall your heavenly Father which is in heaven give good things to them that ask Him?"* This is comparing the willingness of an earthly father to give gifts to his child and how our Godly

23

Father will gladly meet our needs with all good things.

Additionally, Matthew 7:19-20 speaks of recognizing the prophets and false prophets from one another. They can be distinguished, not only of the actions of their lives but the doctrine they proclaim. "Every tree that brings not forth good fruit is hewn down, and cast into the fire. Wherefore *by their fruits ye shall know them.*"

Jesus taught in Matthew 7:22-24 that not everyone who professes Jesus Christ as Lord is truly saved. The genuinely saved person is one that does the will of the Father and is continually living in obedience as a normal course of life. "Not every one that saith, Lord, Lord, shall enter into the kingdom of heaven; *but he that doeth the will (shall enter) of my Father which is in heaven.* Therefore whosoever hears these sayings of Mine and doeth them, *I will liken him unto a wise man, which built his house on a rock.*"

Matthew 13:16-17: *But blessed are your eyes for they see, and your ears for they hear.* For verily I say unto you, that many prophets and righteous men have desired to see those things which ye see, and have not seen them; and hear the things you hear, and have not heard them.
This means that for those who know not the Lord, their hearts are waxed gross (fattened and filled), their ears are dull of hearing, and their eyes have closed.

## THE BLESSING OF THE HOLY SPIRIT

Matthew 21:21: And Jesus said, "Verily I say unto you, *if you have faith and doubt not,* you shall not only do this which is done to the fig tree, but also if ye shall say unto this mountain, be thou removed and be thou cast into the sea, *it shall be done."*

The Disciples are told to fear not because the enemy can only take their physical lives. This cannot prevent their blessed life eternal. Matthew 10:26 says, "Fear them not therefore; for *there is nothing covered that shall not be revealed; and hid, that shall not be known."* And Matthew 10:28 says, "Fear not them which kill the body, *but are not able to kill the soul:* but rather fear Him which is able to destroy both soul and body in hell."

Matthew 10:32: Whosoever shall confess Me before men, *him will I confess also before My Father which is in heaven.*
To confess Jesus is to acknowledge Him before men, confirming your belief, and in so doing, saying, I belong to You!

Matthew 10:33: But whomsoever denies Me before men, *him will I deny before My Father which is in heaven.*
This denial is a lifelong resistance to Christ. This is a refusal to confess Christ at all.

25

Matthew 10:40: He that receiveth you, receiveth Me, and he that receiveth Me, receives Him that sent me.

Matthew 10:41-42: He that receives a prophet in the name of a prophet, shall receive a prophet's reward; and he that receives a righteous man in the name of a righteous man *shall receive a righteous man's reward.* And whosoever shall give a drink unto one of these little ones a cup of *water [the word of God]* only in the name of a disciple, verily I say unto you, he *shall in no wise lose his reward*.

The reward could be to share in the rewards of the prophet by supporting their ministry with works or finances.

Matthew 11: 28-29: Come unto Me all ye that labor and are heavy laden, *and I will give you rest.* Take My yoke upon you, and learn of Me; for I am meek and lowly in heart: *and ye shall find rest unto your souls*.

An invitation from the Lord to seek Him and know of Him for He will give you rest and comfort.

Matthew 12:32: And whosoever speaketh a word against the Son of man, it shall be forgiven him: but *whosoever speaketh against the Holy Ghost, it shall not be forgiven him*, neither in this world, neither in the world to come.

Matthew 12:36: But I say unto you, *that every idle word that men shall speak, they **shall give account***

*thereof* in the day of judgment.
Be mindful of what you speak.

Matthew 13:12: *For whosoever hath, to him shall be given, and he shall have **more abundance**:* but whosoever hath not, from him shall be taken away even what he hath.
This is the work of man's belief or unbelief and rebellion.

Matthew 16:18: And I also say unto thee, that thou art Peter and upon *this rock* I build my church; and *the **gates of hell shall not prevail***.
This rock refers to Jesus, an immovable stone.

Matthew 16:19: And *I will give unto thee the keys of the kingdom* of heaven: and **whatsoever thou shall bind on earth shall be bound in heaven**: and *whatsoever thou shalt loose on earth **shall be loosed in heaven***.
This is not for Peter only, for we have also been promised this same power.

Matthew 16:27: For the Son of man shall come in the glory of His Father with His angels; and then ***He shall reward every man according to his works***.
This refers to the second coming of Jesus Christ, not the rapture: when He receives His faithful church in the air.

Matthew 25:21: Well done thy good and faithful servant: thou has been faithful over a few things, *I will make thee ruler over many things: enter thou unto the joy of thy Lord.*

Mark 4:24: *Take heed, what ye hear: with **what measure ye mete, it shall be measured to you**: and **unto you who hear shall more be given.***
Note:

    a.  Hearing determines your harvest.

    b.  If you don't listen, you lose it.

    c.  If you don't follow instruction, that is a missed opportunity. We are held responsible for what we know. Luke 12:48 says, "But he that knew not, and did commit things worthy of stripes, shall be beaten, with few stripes. For unto whom much is given, to him much shall be required: and to whom men have committed much, of him they will ask the more."

Mark 16:17-18: Jesus said, "And these signs shall follow them that believe, *in My name they shall cast out devils*, they shall speak with new tongues. They shall take up serpents: and if they drink any deadly thing, it shall not hurt them: *they shall lay hands on the sick and they shall recover.*"

Luke 1:73-74: The oath which He swore to our father Abraham, that he would grant unto us, that we being *delivered out of the hand of our enemies*, and from the hand of all that hate us.

Luke 1:79: To give light to them that sit in darkness and in the shadow of death, to *guide our feet into the way of peace*.

Luke 2:10-11: And the angel said unto them, Fear not: for, behold, I bring you *good tidings of great joy*, which shall be to all people, for unto you this day is born a Savior, which is Christ the Lord.

Luke 3:6: And all flesh shall *see the salvation of God.* This is an Old Testament prophecy fulfilled from Isaiah. 40:3-5, for the mouth of the Lord hath spoken it. And all flesh did see His mighty power that glorified God.

Luke 9:56: For the Son of man [Jesus] *is not come to destroy men's lives but to save them.*

Luke 21:15: For *I will give you a mouth and wisdom*, which all your adversaries shall not be able to gainsay nor resist.

Luke 21:36: Watch ye therefore and pray always, that ye pass, and to stand before the Son of man.
Rapture - Be watchful.

John 3:16: For God so loved the world that he gave His only begotten Son, that whosoever believeth in Him shall not perish but have everlasting life.

John 4:14: But whosoever drinketh of the water that I shall give him *shall never thirst*; but the water that I shall give him shall be *in him a well of water springing up into everlasting life*.

John 6:35: I am the bread of life; he that cometh to Me [is fulfilled] **shall never hunger**; and he that believeth on Me **shall never thirst.**

John 6:37: All that the Father giveth to Me shall come to Me; and him that cometh [in faith, repenting, and turning to Me with their whole heart] to Me, *I in no wise will cast out*.

John 6:56-57: He that eateth My flesh and drinketh My blood *dwelleth in Me and I in him*.
Jesus is this bread of life; the bread represents His body and the wine, His blood. We are to do this communion in remembrance of Him.

John 7:16-18: My doctrine is not Mine, but His that sent Me. If any man will do His will, he shall know of the doctrine, whether it be of God, or whether I speak of myself. He that speaketh of himself seeketh his own glory: *but he that seeketh His glory that sent him, the same is true, and no unrighteousness is in him*.

John 14:20: At that day ye shall know that *I Am in My*

*Father, and ye in Me, and I in you.*
This is spiritual union and power.

John 14:26: But the Comforter [this Greek word is *parakletos* which means one called to the side of another to help] which is the Holy Ghost, whom the Father will send in My name, *he shall teach you all things, and bring all things to your remembrance, whatsoever I have said unto you.*
And also John 16:8, "When He is come He will reprove the world of sin, and of righteousness and of judgment."

John 8:12: I Am the Light of the world: *he that followeth Me shall not walk in darkness, but shall have the light of life.*

John 12:26: If any man serve Me, let him follow Me; and where I Am, there shall also My servant be: *if any man serve Me, him will My Father honor.*

John 14:1-3: Let not your hearts be troubled, ye believe in God, believe also in Me. In My Father's house [heaven] are many mansions; if it were not so, I would have told you. *I go to prepare a place for you,* and if I go and prepare a place for you, I will come again, and receive you unto myself: *that where I Am, there ye may be also.*
This is the first picture of the rapture with Jesus returning for the church.

John 14:14: If ye shall *ask anything in My Name*, I will do it.

John 14:21: He that hath My commandments and keepeth them, he it is that loveth Me; and he that loveth Me shall be loved by My Father, and *I will love him and manifest Myself to him.*

John 14:23: If a man love Me, he will keep My words: and My Father will love him, and *We will come unto him, and make our abode with him.*
This is the secret of divine indwelling.

John 15:2, 5: Every branch in Me that beareth not fruit, *He taketh away:* and every *branch that beareth fruit, he purgeth it so it will bring forth more fruit.* I Am the Vine, ye are the branches: he that abideth in Me and I in Him, the same bringeth forth much fruit: for without Me ye can do nothing.

There are two kinds of branches. If the branch is fruitful he will be purged to produce more fruit. One who produces no fruit will be cut away. This is done by the Father. We must remain in Him. He is the True Vine, and we must abide in Him to be saved.

In summary, the promise of the Holy Spirit is power and that power works in us and through us. Consider Mark 9:1 and Acts 1:8: "But you shall receive power, after the Holy Spirit is come upon you." And also

Luke. 24:49, "tarry...until you are endowed with power from on high."

But you shall receive Power,
after the Holy Spirit is come upon you!
And this power is given with power from God!

**Mighty Power, Dynamite Strength Power!**

# *Three*

## THE PROMISE OF SALVATION

Salvation is a gift. As Christians, we should value our salvation above all else, with the anointing coming in at a close second. Salvation means *saved, deliverance from, and preservation from destruction and judgment.* Without salvation, we are doomed to destruction, eternal judgment, and the punishment of Hell.

### THE WAY OF SALVATION

We are saved by our faith in Jesus Christ and what He did for us through His death and resurrection. This is the grace of God towards us and we receive it by faith.

Ephesians 2:8-9: For *by grace are ye saved through faith*; and that not of yourselves: [it is] the gift of God: Not of works, lest any man should boast.

Hebrews11:6: But, without faith it is impossible to please Him: for he who cometh to God *must believe that He is,* and that He is the rewarder of them that diligently seek Him.

The '**Romans Road**' is a way of explaining the good news through scripture. Read the following verses (one at a time) from the New Testament book of Romans out loud, even if you can only whisper. After each verse, consider what the word/verse says to you. When you speak it, God will open your ears, eyes, and heart to His Word.

1. Romans 3:23: For all have sinned and come short of the glory of God.
   - What does this verse say to you?

2. Romans 3:10: There is none righteous, no not one.
   - What does this verse say to you?

3. Romans 6:23: For the wages of sin is death; but the gift of God is eternal life…
   - What does this verse say to you?

4. Romans 10:9: if thou confess with thy mouth the Lord Jesus, and shall believe in thine heart that God hath raised Him from the dead, thy shall be saved.
   - What does this verse say to you?

5. Romans 10:13: For whosoever shall call upon the name of the Lord shall be saved.
   - What does this verse say to you?

6. Romans 5:1: Therefore, being justified by faith, we have peace with God through our Lord Jesus Christ.

   • What does this say to you?

7. Romans 8:1: There is therefore now no condemnation to them which are in Christ Jesus, who walk not after the flesh, but after the Spirit.

   • What does this verse say to you?

God loves you and has a plan for your life. (John 3:16.) For God so loved the world *[the world includes you]*, that he gave his only begotten Son, that **whosoever believeth in him** should not perish, but have everlasting life.

## MORE PROMISES OF YOUR SALVATION

1 Corinthians 15:3b-4: Christ died for our sins, according to the Scriptures; and that He was buried and **He rose again** the third day according to scripture.

John 10:10b: I am come that they may have life, and have it more abundantly.

John 14:6: Jesus said, "I Am the way, the truth and the life, **no man cometh unto the Father but by Me**."

John 1:12: But, as many as received Him, **to them gave**

*He power* to become sons of God, even them who believe in His name…

Acts 16:31: Believe on the Lord and *you shall be saved, and thy house.*

Ephesians 2:8: For by grace are ye saved, through faith; and that not yourselves: *it is a gift of God.*

1 Peter 2:9: But you are a chosen generation a royal priesthood, a holy nation, peculiar people; that ye should show forth the praises of *him who hath called you out of darkness and into his marvelous light.*

Luke 1:71: That we should be *saved from our enemies*, and from the hand of all that hate us.

Acts 13:26: Men and brethren, children of the stock of Abraham, and whosoever among you feareth God, *to you is the word of this salvation*.

Romans 1:16: For I am not ashamed of the gospel of Jesus Christ: for *it is the power of God unto salvation to every one that believeth*; to the Jew first, and also to the Greek.

Ephesians 1:13: In whom ye also trusted, after that ye heard the word of truth, *the gospel of your salvation*: in whom also after that ye believed, *ye were sealed with that Holy Spirit of promise.*

## Salvation from Sin

Luke 1:77: To give *knowledge of salvation* unto his people **by the remission of their sins**.

Luke 19:9: And Jesus said unto him, *"This day is salvation come to this house*, for so much as he also is a son of Abraham."

Romans 10:10: For *with the heart man believeth unto righteousness*; and *with the mouth confession is made* **unto salvation**.

2 Thessalonians 2:13: But we are bound to give thanks always to God for you, brethren beloved of the Lord, because *God hath from the beginning chosen you to salvation* through sanctification of the Spirit and belief of the truth.

# Four

## PROMISES OF BODILY HEALING

A very important element of Jesus' earthly ministry was healing the sick. Jesus stood up in the Synagogue on the Sabbath to read: "*The Spirit of the Lord is **upon Me*** [the Spirit upon someone indicates His moving to do some supernatural work] *because He has **anointed Me to preach** the gospel to the poor* [give the good news to the poor, destitute, needy] *and deliverance to captives* [those in sin, sickness and death; to heal: the broken heart, mind, soul and body, those in darkness.] (See also Luke 4:18; and Acts 10:38; Ephesians 4:8-10; Hebrews 2:14-15.)

For us to receive this healing for ourselves through our faith in Jesus, **we must give voice to His Word with our mouth. This is the language of health to our body**. Just as we take medicine into our body to aid in physical healing, in the same manner, we must receive God's Word into our spirit for supernatural healing. There is Power in the Word of God.

*Pray:*
*Father, I cannot heal myself, but You have given*
*me the grace and ability to receive healing.*
*Through faith in Your Word, the power of the*
*Holy Spirit and the glorious name of Jesus, I*
*proclaim I am already healed.*
*Devil, I bind you by the power of the Holy*
*Spirit, and in the name of Jesus, I command you*
*to leave my body, now!*

## NEW TESTAMENT HEALING PROMISES BY BOOK

All who had come to Jesus for healing in the first four gospels were completely healed. Jesus said, the same power He had, this same power has been given to us.

### Matthew

Matthew 8:3: And Jesus put forth His hand, and touched him (the man with leprosy), saying, I will; be thou clean. And immediately, his leprosy was clean.

Matthew 8:16-17: They brought unto Jesus many with devils: and He *cast out the spirits with His Word* and **healed all** *that* were sick: That it might be fulfilled which was spoken by Isaiah [53:4] the prophet, saying, *"Himself took our infirmities, and bare our sicknesses."*

Matthew 9:29-30: Then He touched their eyes, saying

42

*according to your faith*, be it unto you. And their eyes were opened.

Matthew 9:35: And Jesus went about all the cities and villages, teaching…and preaching…and *healing every sickness and every disease among the people*.

Matthew 12:15: Great multitudes followed Him, and *He healed them all*.

Matthew 10:8: *Heal the sick, cleanse the lepers, raise the dead, cast out devils*: freely you have received, freely give.
This was the command Jesus gave to His disciples, and it is the same for us as His disciples today.

Matthew 13:15: When they understand with their heart and believe, "they should be converted and *I should heal them all*."

Matthew 14:14: And Jesus went forth, and saw a great multitude, and was moved with compassion toward them, and *He healed their sick*.

Matthew 14:36: And besought Him that they might only touch the hem of His garment: and *as many as touched were made perfectly whole*.

Matthew 15:30-31: And great multitudes came unto Him, having with them those that were lame, blind, dumb, maimed, and many others, and cast them down At Jesus' feet; and ***He healed them***: Insomuch that the multitude wondered when they saw the dumb speak, the maimed to be made whole, the lame to walk, and the blind to see: *and they glorified the God of Israel.*

Matthew 17:20: If you have faith as a grain of mustard seed, ye shall say unto this mountain, remove hence to yonder place; and it shall remove; and *nothing shall be impossible unto you.*

Matthew 18:18: *Whatever you bind on earth shall have been bound in heaven*; and whatever you loose on earth shall have been loosed in heaven.

Matthew 18:19-20: Again I say to you, that if two of you agree on earth about anything that they may *ask, it shall be done for them by My Father who is in heaven.* For where two or three are gathered together in My name, I am there in their midst.

Matthew 21:22: And all things, *whatsoever ye shall ask in prayer, believing, ye shall receive.*

**Mark**

Mark 9:23: Jesus said unto him, "If thou can believe, *all things are possible to him that believe."*

Mark 5:34: Daughter, *thy faith hath made thee whole.*

Mark 11:23: For verily I say unto you, that *whosoever shall say unto this mountain [sickness/problem]* be thou removed, and be cast into the sea; and shall not doubt in his heart, but shall believe that those things which *he saith* shall come to pass; he shall have whatsoever.

This tells us to give voice to our faith by speaking to our problem in the name of Jesus.

## Luke

Luke 4:18: The Spirit of the Lord is upon me, because he has anointed me to preach the gospel to the poor, *he hath sent me to heal the broken hearted, to preach deliverance to the captives and recovering of sight to the blind, to set at liberty them that are bruised.*

Luke 6:10: He said unto the man, "Stretch forth thy hand." And He did so: and his hand was *restored whole* as the other.

## John

John 14:12: Verily, verily [truly, truly] I say unto you, he that believeth on Me, *the works that I do shall he do also; and greater works* than these shall he do; because I go unto my Father.

Jesus is interceding for us at His Father's right hand.

John 10:10: I [Jesus] am come *that they might have*

45

*life*, and that they might *have it [life] more abundantly*.

*Pray*
*Thank You Lord Jesus that You have given me*
*abundant life. I receive that life through Your*
*Word and it flows to every organ of my body,*
*bringing healing and health.*

## Romans

Romans 6:14: For *sin [and sickness] shall not have dominion over you*: for ye are not under the law but under grace.

## Philippians

Philippians 4:6: Be careful [or anxious] for nothing; but in everything by prayer and supplication with thanksgiving. *Let your request be made known unto God.*

## 1 Peter

1 Peter 2:24: Who His own self bare our sins in His own body on the tree, that we, being dead to sins, should live unto righteousness: **by whose stripes ye [we] were healed.**

1 Peter 5:7 *Casting all your care upon Him*; for He careth for you.

## James

James 4:7 Submit yourselves therefore to God. *Resist the devil, and he will flee from you.*

James 1:21 receive with meekness the engrafted word, *which is able to save the soul.*

## 1Timothy

1 Timothy 1:7 For God has not given us a spirit of fear; but of *power, and of a sound mind.*

## 1 John

1 John 5:4 For *whatsoever is born of God overcometh the world*: and this is the victory that overcometh the world, even our faith.

## 3 John

3 John 1:2 It is my will that *all should prosper and be in health* just as your soul prospers.

## Revelation

Revelation 12:11 And they overcame him [demons, devil, powers of this world] *by the blood of the Lamb and by the Word of their testimony.*

## *Pray this Prayer:*

*Father, each of these verses from your Word have been spoken and have entered my body, they have entered my soul and have filled my spirit.*

*These words are being formed in my body and are nourishing my organs, cells, glands, nerves, bones, muscles, joints, ligaments while bringing strength and healing to areas where needed.*

*I pray in the name of Jesus, giving all honor, glory and praise to your holy name.*

*Thank You, Jesus, for Your Word, and for setting me free. I am not just healed, but I am made whole, without scar or blemish.*

*I Praise God forever!  Amen*

# *Five*

## ADDITIONAL PROMISES
## OF THE NEW TESTAMENT

When you read the word of God, ask the Holy Spirit in the name of Jesus, to bring all the things of God to your remembrance, and He will. For it is His promise to you!

*The Holy Ghost whom the Father shall send in my name [Jesus] he shall teach you all things, and bring all things to your remembrance, whatsoever I have said unto you. (John.14:26.)*

### MATTHEW, MARK, LUKE, JOHN

Matthew 1:21: And she [Mary] shall bring forth a Son, and thou shalt call His name JESUS: for He shall save *His people* [denotes one's own populace.]

Matthew 3:11: I indeed baptize you with water unto repentance: but he that cometh after me is mightier than I whose shoes I am not worthy to bear: *he shall baptize you with the Holy Ghost and with fire.*

He will burn the chaff with unquenchable fire.

Matthew 7:21: Not every one that saith unto Me, Lord, Lord, shall enter into the kingdom of heaven: But *he who do the will of My Father which is in heaven.*

Matthew 5:3: Blessed are the poor in spirit, for *theirs is the kingdom of heaven.*

Matthew 5:5: Blessed are the meek for *they shall inherit the earth.*

Matthew 5:6: Blessed are they which do hunger and thirst after righteousness for *they shall be filled.*
Righteousness is justification, equity of character.

Matthew 5:7: Blessed are the merciful for *they shall obtain mercy.*
Mercy means compassion.

Matthew 5:8: Blessed are the pure of heart, *for they shall see God.*

Matthew 5:9: Blessed are the peacemakers for *they shall be called the children of God.*
Children of God means kinship, sonship.

Matthew 5:10: Blessed are they which are persecuted for righteousness sake: for *theirs is the kingdom of heaven.*

Matthew 6:4: That thy alms may be in secret: and thy Father which seeth in secret *himself shall reward thee openly.*

Matthew 5:14: Ye are the light of the world, *A city that sets on a hill cannot be hid.*

Matthew 5:19: Whosoever shall break one of these least commandments, and shall teach men so, he shall be called the least in the kingdom of heaven: *but whosoever shall do and teach them, the same shall be called great in the kingdom of heaven.*

A promise given by Jesus is victory of temptation. "Man shall not live by bread alone, but by every word that proceeds out of the mouth of God." (Matthew. 4:4; Luke 4:4.) Jesus said in John 4:32, "I have meat to eat that ye know not of." His source of strength was always **obedience to the Father's will,** *this* **obedience is our strength** *as well.*

In Matthew 4:19, Jesus speaks to His fishermen disciples, saying, *"Follow Me and I will **make you fishers of men**."* And they followed him. They became Evangelists with soul-winning power.

Matthew 10:8: *Heal the sick, cleanse the lepers, raise the dead, cast out devils:* freely you have received, freely give.

Matthew 18:4-5: Whosoever therefore shall *humble himself as this little child. The same is greatest in the Kingdom of heaven.* And, whosoever shall receive one such child in My Name receives Me.

In Matthew 6:30, it teaches that God is not only our Creator but promises to be our sustainer. "Wherefore, if God so clothe the grass of the field, which today is, and tomorrow is cast into the oven, *shall he not much more clothe you*, O ye of little faith?"

Matthew 7:7: **Ask,** *and it shall be given you;* **seek,** *and you shall find;* **knock,** *and it shall be opened unto you.*

Matthew 7:11: If you then, being evil, know how to give good gifts unto your children, *how much more shall your heavenly Father which is in heaven give good things to them that ask Him?*

Matthew 7:22, 24: Not every one that saith, Lord, Lord, shall enter into the kingdom of heaven; *but he that doeth the will (shall enter) of my Father which is in heaven.* Therefore whosoever hear, these sayings of mine, and doeth them, *I will liken him unto a wise man, which built his house on a rock.*

Matthew 8:15 tells how Peter's mother-in-law was healed because of faith.

Matthew 8:16-17: When evening had come they brought unto him [Jesus] many that were possessed with devils; *and he cast out the spirits with His word and healed all that were sick; that it might be fulfilled which was spoken by Isaiah the prophet, saying Himself **[Jesus] took our infirmities, and bare our sicknesses.***

Matthew 9:29-30: Then touched He their eyes, saying, *"**According to your faith be it unto you.**"* And their eyes were opened:
They had put their faith in Him as the Messiah, calling Him the son of David when they cried out for His help.

Matthew 13:16-17: *But blessed are your eyes for they see, and your ears for they hear.* For verily I say unto you, that many prophets and righteous men have desired to see those things which ye see, and have not seen them; and hear the things you hear, and have not heard them.

Matthew 21:21: And Jesus said, "Verily I say unto you, ***if you have faith and doubt not,*** *you shall not only do this which is done to the fig tree, but also if ye shall say unto this mountain, be thou removed and be thou cast into the sea, **it shall be done.**"*

Matthew 10:26: Fear them not therefore; for ***there is nothing covered that shall not be revealed; and hid, that shall not be known.***

53

Matthew 10:28: Fear not them which kill the body, *but are not able to kill the soul:* but rather fear him which is able to destroy both soul and body in hell.

Matthew 10:32: Whosoever shall confess me before men*, him will I confess also before My Father which is in heaven.*
To confess is to acknowledge Jesus before men, confirming your belief, and in so doing, saying, I belong to You, Jesus!

Matthew 10:33: But whomsoever denies Me before men, *him will I deny before My Father which is in heaven.*
This denial is a lifelong resistance to Christ. This is a refusal to confess Christ at all.

Matthew 10:40: He that receiveth you receiveth Me, and he that receiveth Me, receives Him that sent me.

Matthew 10:41-42: He that receives a prophet in the name of a prophet, shall receive a prophet's reward; and he that receives a righteous man in the name of a righteous man *shall receive a righteous man's reward.* And whosoever shall give a drink unto one of these little ones a cup of *water (the word of God)* only in the name of a disciple, verily I say unto you, he *shall in no wise lose his reward*.
The reward could be to share in the prophet's rewards by supporting their ministry with works or finances.

Matthew 11:28-29: Come unto Me all ye that labor and are heavy laden, ***and I will give you rest.*** Take My yoke upon you, and learn of Me; for I am meek and lowly in heart: ***and ye shall find rest unto your souls***.
This is an invitation from the Lord to seek Him and know of Him for He will give you rest and comfort.

Matthew 12:32: And whosoever speaketh a word against the Son of man, it shall be forgiven him: but *whosoever speaketh against the Holy Ghost, **it shall not be forgiven him**,* neither in this world, neither in the world to come.

Matthew 12:36: But I say unto you, *that every idle word that men shall speak, they **shall give account thereof** in the day of judgment.*
Be mindful of what you speak.

Matthew 13:12: *For whosoever hath, to him shall be given, and he shall have **more abundance***: but whosoever hath not, from him shall be taken away even that he hath.
This is the work of man's belief or unbelief and rebellion.

Matthew 16:18-19: And Jesus said unto him [Peter] that thou art Peter and upon *this rock* I build my church; and ***the gates of hell shall not prevail***. And *I will give unto thee the keys of the kingdom* of heaven: and ***whosoever thou shall bind on earth shall be*** *bound in heaven*: and *whatsoever thou shalt loose on earth* **shall be loosed in heaven**.

This rock refers to Jesus (the Greek word *petra*), an immovable stone. This is not for Peter only, for we have also been promised this same power.

Matthew 16:27: For the Son of man shall come in the glory of His Father with His angels; and then ***He shall reward every man according to his works***.

This refers to the second coming, not the rapture.

Matthew 6:14-15: For if ye forgive men their trespasses, *your heavenly Father will also forgive you:* but if you forgive not men their trespasses, neither will your Father forgive your trespasses.

Matthew 6:19-21: Lay not up for yourself treasures upon earth, where moth and rust doth corrupt, and where thieves break through and steal: ***But lay up for yourselves treasures in heaven,*** *where neither moth nor rust doth corrupt, and where* thieves do not break through nor steal ***For where your treasure is, there will your heart be also.***

Matthew 6:30: Wherefore if God so clothe the grass of the field, which today is and tomorrow is cast into the oven, *shall He not much more clothe you,* O ye of little faith.

Matthew 7:7-8: Ask, and it shall be given you: seek,

and ye shall find; knock, and it shall be opened unto you: for *every one that asketh, receiveth, and he that seeketh, findeth and to him that knocketh, it shall be opened.*

Matthew 11:28: ***Come*** unto me all ye who are heavy laden and ***I will give you rest.***
*Come*, was the Lord's general invitation to man.

## Mark

Mark 4:24: Take heed, what ye hear: with what measure ye mete, it shall be measured to you: and ***unto you who hear shall more be given***.
This means that (a) Hearing determines your harvest (b) If you don't listen, you lose it.

Mark 16:15-16: Go ye into all the world and preach the gospel to every creature. ***He that believeth and is baptized shall be saved***: but he that believeth not shall be damned.

Mark 16:17-18: Jesus said, "And these signs shall follow them that believe, In My Name they shall cast out devils, they shall speak with new tongues. They shall take up serpents: and if they drink any deadly thing, it shall not hurt them: they shall ***lay hands on the sick, and they shall recover."***

57

## Luke

Luke 1:32-33: He [Jesus] shall be great, and shall be called the Son of the Highest: and the Lord God shall give unto Him the throne of His father David, and He shall reign over the house of Jacob forever; and *of His kingdom there shall be no end.*

Luke 1:73-74: The oath which He sware to our father Abraham, that he would grant unto us, that *we being delivered out of the hand of our enemies, and from the hand of all that hate us.*

Luke 1:79: To give light to them that sit in darkness and in the shadow of death, *to guide our feet into the way of peace.*

Luke 2:10-11: And the angel said unto them, Fear not: for, behold, *I bring you good tidings of great joy, which shall be to all people*

## John

John 3:16-17: For God so loved the world that He gave His only begotten Son, that whosoever *believeth in Him* shall not perish but *have everlasting life.* For God sent not His Son into the world to condemn the world: but that the world *through Him might be saved.*

John 4:14: But *whosoever drinketh of the water that I*

*shall give him shall never_thirst*; But the water that I shall give him, shall be in him a well of water springing up unto everlasting life.

John 5:28-29: Marvel not at this: for the hour is coming, in that *all that are in the graves shall hear His voice,* and shall come forth, they that have done good, unto the resurrection of life.

John 6:37: All that the Father giveth Me, shall come to Me; and him that cometh to Me *I will in no wise cast out.*

John 8:12: I am the light of the world, he that followeth Me shall not walk in darkness, but *shall have the light of life.*

John 14:18: I will not leave you comfortless; *I will come to you.*

John 14:21: He that hath my commandments, and keepeth them, he it is that loveth Me: and he that loveth Me shall be loved by My Father, and *I will love him, and will manifest Myself to him.*

John 8:32: And you shall know the truth and *the truth shall make you free.*

John14:13-14: And whatsoever you shall ask in My name, that will I do, that the Father may be glorified in the Son. *If you ask anything in my name, I will do it.*

John 16:23: And in that day (day of going back to the Father) you shall ask me nothing. Verily, verily, I say unto you. Whatsoever ye shall ask the Father in My Name, He will give it you.
This means that all prayer is prayed to the Father, in the name of the Son, and the Son will give the Father all glory, and *we shall be given our request.*

John 15:7: If you abide in Me, and My Words abide in you, *ye shall ask what ye will, and it shall be done unto you.*

## ACTS, ROMANS, 1&2 CORINTHIANS

Acts 10:43: To Him give all the prophets witness, that through His Name, *whosoever believeth in Him shall receive remission of sins.*

Acts 3:20-21: And *He shall send Jesus Christ*, which before was preached unto you whom the heaven must receive until the times of restitution of all things, [the second coming of Jesus] which God has spoken by the mouth of all His holy prophets since the world began.

Acts 1:8: *But ye shall receive power* after that the Holy Ghost has come upon you:

Acts 20:32: And now brethren I commend you to God,

and to the word of His grace which is able to **build you up, and to give you an inheritance** among all them which are sanctified.

Our body, soul and spirit is able to be repaired and made new again. The Word within us, the gospel of grace builds us up.

Acts 13:38-39: Be it known unto you therefore, men and brethren, that through this man is preached unto you **the forgiveness of sins**: and **by Him all that believe are justified** by all things, from which ye could not be justified by the Law of Moses.

This means that Jesus paid the price for man's redemption.

Acts 26:17: Delivering you from the people [Jews] and Gentiles, unto whom I send you, to open their eyes the power of satan unto God, that they may **receive forgiveness of sins, and inheritance among them which are Sanctified by Faith that is in Me.**

## Romans

Romans 2:4b: The goodness of God *leadeth thee to repentance*.

Romans 5:5: I forgive others as Christ has forgiven me, for *the love of God is shed abroad in my heart* by the Holy Ghost which is given unto us.

Romans 10:17: So then, *faith cometh by hearing*, and hearing by the Word of God.

Romans 2:10:11: But *glory, honor and peace to every man that worketh good*, to the Jew first and also to the Gentile. For there is no respect of person, with God.

Romans 3:22-24: Even the righteousness of God which is by faith of Jesus Christ unto all and upon all them that believe: for there is no difference. For *all have sinned and come short of the glory of God; Being justified freely by His grace, through the redemption that is in Christ Jesus.*

Romans 3:30: Seeing it is one God, which shall justify the *circumcision* **by** *faith and uncircumcision* **through** *faith.*

Romans 5: 8-9: But God commendeth His love toward us, in that, while we were yet sinners, Christ died for us. Much more than *being now justified by His blood.*

Romans 5:17: ...how much more they that *receive abundance of grace and of the gift of righteousness* shall reign in life by one, Jesus Christ.

Romans 5:20: But where sin abounded, *grace much more abound.*

Romans 6:5: For if we have been planted together in

the likeness of His death, we shall be also in the *likeness of His resurrection*:

Romans 8:26: Likewise **the Spirit also helpeth our infirmities**: for if we know not what we should pray for as we ought: but the Spirit itself *maketh intercession for us with groanings which cannot be uttered.*

Romans 10:4: For Christ is the end of the law, for **righteousness to every one who believeth**.

Romans 10:9-10: That if thou shalt **confess with thy mouth the Lord Jesus, and shall believe in thine heart that God hath raised him from the dead**, *thou shall be saved.*

Romans 15:13: Now the God of hope fill you with all joy and peace in believing, that ye may **abound in hope, through the power of the Holy Ghost**.

## 1 Corinthians

1 Corinthians 1:7-8: *So that ye come behind in no gift*; waiting for the coming of our Lord and Savior. *Who shall also confirm you* unto the end, *that ye may be blameless in the day of our Lord Jesus Christ.*

1 Corinthians 1:30: But of him are **ye in Christ Jesus**, Who of God is made unto us **wisdom, and right-**

*eousness, and sanctification, and redemption.*

1 Corinthians 3:20-21: And again, *The Lord knoweth the thoughts of the wise, that they are vain.* Therefore *let no man glory in men.* For *all things are yours.*

1 Corinthians 12:8-11: For to one is given by the Spirit the word of wisdom; to another the word of knowledge by the same Spirit; To another faith by the same Spirit; to another the gifts of healing by the same Spirit; to another the working of miracles; and another discerning of spirits; to another divers kind of tongues; to another the interpretation of tongues: *But all these worketh that one and the selfsame Spirit, dividing to every man severally as he will.*

1 Corinthians 12:13: For by one Spirit are we all *baptized* into one body, whether we be Jew or Gentiles, whether we be bond or free, and *have been all made free to drink into one Spirit.*

1 Corinthians 15:26: The last *enemy that shall be destroyed is death.*

## 2 Corinthians

2 Corinthians 1:20: For **all the promises of God in Him are yea, and in Him** Amen.

2 Corinthians 3:17: Now, the Lord is that Spirit: and

*where the Spirit of the Lord is, there shall be liberty*.

2 Corinthians 3:18: But we all, with open face beholding as in a glass the glory of the Lord, *are changed into the same image from glory to glory, even as by the Spirit of the Lord.*

2 Corinthians 4:16-17: For that which cause we faint not; but though our outward man perish, yet the *inward man is renewed day by day*. For our light affliction, which is but for a moment, *worketh for us a far more exceeding and eternal weight of glory*.

2 Corinthians 5:17-18: Therefore, **if any man be in Christ he is a new creature**: [old things,the spirit nature, the power of sin and transgressions] are passed away; behold *all things are become new* [reconciling man to himself, that man may become righteous.]

2 Corinthians 6:16: And what agreement hath the temple of God with idols? For *ye are the temple of the living God*; as God has said, "I will dwell in them, and walk in them; and I will be their God, and they shall be My people."

2 Corinthians 6:17-18: Wherefore come out from among them [unclean and foul spirits and the world and its ways], and be ye separate, saith the Lord, and touch not the unclean thing; and *I will receive you, and will be a Father unto you.*

God, who owns all and rules all will assume all responsibility of parental concern and give Himself to the eternal care of His family, and ye shall be my sons and daughters, saith the Lord Almighty. Praise God!

2 Corinthians 8:9: For ye know the grace of our Lord Jesus Christ, that though He was rich, yet for your sake became poor, that *you through His poverty might be rich*.

2 Corinthians 9:6: But this I say, he which soweth sparingly shall reap sparingly; and *he which soweth bountifully shall reap bountifully.*

2 Corinthians 9:8: And *God is able to make all grace abound toward you; that ye always have all sufficiency in all things*, and may abound to every good work.

2 Corinthians 9:10-11: Now he that ministereth seed to the sower both minister bread for your food and multiply your seed sown, and increase the fruit of your righteousness. *Being enriched in everything to all bountifulness*, which causeth through us thanksgiving to God.

2 Corinthians 10:4-5: For the weapons of our warfare are not carnal, but mighty through God to the pulling down of strongholds. Casting down imaginations and every high thing that exhalteth itself against the knowledge of God, and bringing into captivity every

thought to the obedience of Christ [we stand ready at all times, taking every thought prisoner, and lead it into captivity to obey Christ. Bringing down all that is contrary to purity, virtue and righteousness.]

2 Corinthians 12:9: And Jesus said to Paul, "*My grace is sufficient for thee*: for my strength is made perfect in weakness." Most gladly, therefore, will I rather glory in my infirmities, that the power of Christ may rest upon me.

2 Corinthians 13:4: For though he was crucified through weakness [without strength], yet he liveth by the power [dunamis, capability, ability] of God. For we also are weak in him, but we shall live with him by the power of God toward you. [His seeming weakness became his strength, he seemed powerless to help himself, but the power of God was within him as it is with us.]

## GALATIANS, EPHESIANS, PHILIPPIANS, COLOSSIANS

Galatians 1:4: *Who gave himself for our sins*, that he might *deliver us from this present evil world*, according to the will of God and our Father.

Galatians 3:14: That the blessing of Abraham might come on the Gentiles through Jesus Christ, *that we may receive the promise of the Spirit through faith*.

Galatians 3:29: And if ye be Christ's then are ye Abraham's seed [something sown, sperm] and heirs according to the promise [a pledge, a divine assurance of good.]

Galatians 4:5-7: To redeem them that were under the law, that we might receive the adoption of sons and because we are sons, God hath sent forth the Spirit of His Son into your hearts, crying Abba, Father. Wherefore thou art no more a servant, but a son; and if a son, then an heir [inheritor, benefactor] of God through Christ [Messiah, Anointed One.]

Galatians 5:21: Envyings, murders, drunkenness, reveling (rioting), and such like: of the which I tell you before, as I have also told you in time past, that they which do such things *shall not inherit the kingdom of God.*

## Ephesians

Ephesians 1:7, 14: In whom we have *redemption through his blood*, the *forgiveness of sins*, according to the riches of grace... *Which is the earnest of our inheritance* until the redemption of the purchased possession, unto the praise of his glory.

Ephesians 1:11: In whom *we have obtained an inheritance* being predestinated according to the purpose of him who worketh all things after the counsel of his own will.

Ephesians 1:13: In whom ye also trusted, after that ye heard the word of truth, the gospel of your salvation in whom also ye believed *ye were sealed with the Holy Spirit of promise.*

Ephesians 2:19: Now, therefore, ye are no more strangers and foreigners,[opposed] *but fellow citizens with the saints, and of the household [His own] of God.*

Ephesians 3:20, 21: Now unto *Him Who is able to do exceeding abundantly above all that we ask or think,* according to the power that worketh in us. Unto him be glory, in the church [congregation, members/saints] by Christ Jesus, throughout all ages, world without end. Amen.

Ephesians 4:30: And grieve not the Holy Spirit of God, *whereby ye are sealed* [a private mark, a signet ring, for security, for preservation, to attest] unto the day of redemption [ransom in full, deliverance, redemption.]

Ephesians 5:26: That *he might sanctify and cleanse [to clean, to purify] it with washing of water by the word* [rhema, an utterance] live long on the earth.

Ephesians 6:2-3: Honor thy father and mother; which is the first commandment with promise; *That it may be well with thee, and thou may live long on the earth.* [The whole of the terrene globe, ground, land, world.]

## Philippians

Philippians 4:7: And the *peace of God which passes all understanding [intellect] shall keep your hearts [feelings] and minds* [thoughts] through Christ Jesus.

Philippians 4:19: But my *God shall supply all your needs* according to his riches in glory by Christ Jesus.

## HEBREWS, JAMES, 1&2 PETER

Hebrews 1:14: Are they not all ministering [public servant] spirit [divine, rational soul], sent forth to *minister for them who shall be heirs* of salvation? [deliverance, rescue.]

Hebrews 2:18: For in that He Himself hath suffered being tempted, *He is able to Succor (aid) them that are tempted.*

Hebrews 3:14: For *we are made partakers of Christ*, if we hold the beginning of our confidence steadfast unto the end.

Hebrews 4:16: Let us, therefore, come boldly unto the throne of grace, that we may *obtain mercy and find grace to find help in time of need.*

Hebrews 7:25: Wherefore He is able also to save them to the uttermost that come unto God by Him, seeing He ever liveth to *make intercession, for them.*

Hebrews 8:6: But now hath He obtained a more excellent ministry. By how much also He is the mediator of a *better covenant, which was established upon better promises.*

Hebrews 9:24: For Christ is not entered into the Holy places made with hands [tabernacles] which are the figures (copies)of the true; but into heaven itself, *now to appear in the presence of God for us.*
Christ entered into the Most Holy Place in heaven itself, not a temple made by man's hands.]

Hebrews 11:40: God having provided some *better thing for us* [the promise] that they without us should not be made perfect [those without the promise.]

**James**

James 5:15: And *the prayer of faith shall save the sick,* and the Lord shall raise him up; and if he has committed sins, they shall be forgiven.

**1 Peter**

1 Peter 2:24-25: Who His own self [Jesus] *bare our sins* in His own body on the tree, that we being dead to

sins, should live unto righteousness: *By Whose stripes ye were healed*. For ye were as sheep going astray; but are now *returned unto the Shepherd and Bishop [overseer] of your souls.*

1 Peter 5:4: And when the chief Shepherd shall appear, *ye shall receive a crown of glory that fadeth not away.* [This crown of Glory is promised to faithful pastors, and this is to take place when Jesus returns for His church.]

## 2 Peter

2 Peter 1:2-3: Grace and peace be multiplied unto you through the knowledge of God, and of Jesus our Lord. *According as His divine power hath given unto us all things that pertain unto life and godliness, through the knowledge of Him that hath called us to glory and virtue [moral excellence.]*

2 Peter 1:10: Wherefore the rather, brethren give diligence to make your calling and election sure: *for if you do these things, you shall never fall [stumble.]*

2 Peter 3:13: Nevertheless we, *according to His promise, look for new heavens and a new earth,* wherein dwelleth righteousness.
Look beyond this present world.

## 1, 2, & 3 JOHN, REVELATION

1 John 1:7: But if we walk in the light, as He is in the light, *we have fellowship one with another, and the blood of Jesus Christ his Son cleanseth us from all sin.* Walk in God for He is the light, and live free from bondage.

1 John 2:1-2: My little children, these things write I unto you, that ye sin not. And if any man sin, we have an advocate with the Father, Jesus Christ the Righteous. *And He is the propitiation [an atoning sacrifice] for our sins*: and not for ours only, *but also for the sins of the whole world.*

### *Love is the dominant characteristic true believers.*

1 John 4:17: Herein is our love made perfect, that we may have boldness in the day of judgment: *because so as He is, so are we in this world.*
We have a fearless assurance that if we love in this world as He loves, we need not fear the coming judgment.

1 John 5:10-11: He that believeth on the Son of God, *hath the witness in himself*: he that believeth not God hath made him a liar; because he believeth not the record that God gave of His Son. And this is the record that God has given to us, *eternal life, and this life is in His Son.*

*The assurance of the believer is not based on feelings but on the principles of God's word.*

1 John 5:14-15: And this is the confidence we have in Him, that *if we ask **anything according to His will, He heareth us*:** And if we know that He hears us, whatsoever we ask, *we know we have the petition that we desired of Him.*

*Effectual prayer is according to His will*

## Revelation

Revelation 1:3: ***Blessed*** is he that *readeth* and they that *hear* the words of this prophecy (the Revelation of Jesus Christ), and *keep* those things that are written therein: for the time is at hand.

*Read the Word - Hear the Word - Keep the Word*

Revelation 2:7: He that hath an ear, let him hear what the Spirit saith unto the churches; *To him that overcometh, will I give to eat of the tree of life, which is in the midst of the paradise of God.*

### PROMISES FOR OVERCOMERS

What does it mean to be an overcomer? The Greek word means: to him who gains the victory or is a conqueror. The Apostle Paul said in Romans 6:14,

"For sin should not have dominion over you." So, we should ask ourselves, have we overcome the sin in our life?

We are not able to overcome or have this victory on our own. We must surrender ourselves to the Holy Spirit, giving our free will to him, our mind and our heart. In Romans 8:1-2, the believer is admonished to "walk after the Spirit." We must believe in the cross and have faith in the finished work. The Bible does not teach a sinless perfection, but it does teach victory over sin. Be faithful and confess Him, for this is the victory that overcometh the world even our faith. (1 John 5:4.) Seek not the things of this world.

Hear what the Spirit saith unto the Churches and Promises to the Overcomers in the Book of Revelation:

1. The Tree of Life (v. 2:7.)
2. The Crown of life (v. 2:10; 3:11.)
3. Escape the second death (v.2:11; 20:14.)
4. The hidden manna (v. 2:17.)
5. A new name and a white stone (v. 2:17.)
6. The rapture (v. 2:25; 3:11; plus 1 Thessalonians 4:16; Philippians 4:21.)
7. Power over the nations. (v. 2:26-27.)
8. Defeat of rebels (v.2:27) and the Morning Star (v. 2:28.)

*Revelation 22:2: In the midst of the street of it [New Jerusalem], and on either side of the river, was there the Tree of Life, which bare twelve manner of fruits, and yielded her fruit every month: and the leaves of the tree was for the healing of the nations.*

*Revelation 22:6: And he said unto me, these sayings are faithful and true: and the Lord God of the holy prophets sent his angel to shew unto his servants the things which shortly must be done.*

*Revelation 22:12-13: And behold I come quickly; and My reward is with Me, to give every man according as his work shall be. I am Alpha and Omega, the beginning and the end, the first and the Last.*

*Revelation 22:16: I, Jesus, have sent My angel to testify unto you these things in the churches. I Am the root and the offspring of David, and the Bright and Morning Star.*

**This invitation is for all men to repent and be saved!**

**Surely I Come Quickly!**

# *Six*

## PROMISES FOR REBELS

**Let it be known**: "No sinner is a partaker of the Holy Ghost." (Romans 8:9-16.)

The Holy Ghost cannot be a partner nor associate with the ungodly. Jesus said in John 14:17, "Even the Spirit of truth; whom the world cannot receive, because he seeth Him not, neither knoweth Him…"

### EXAMPLES OF JUDGEMENT

Jude 5: I will, therefore, put you in remembrance, though ye once knew this, how that the Lord, having saved the people out of the land of Egypt, *afterward [fallen from grace], destroyed them that believed not.*

Jude 6: And the angels which kept not their first estate, but left their own habitation [their home with God to dwell in the human sphere], *He hath reserved in everlasting chains under darkness unto the judgment of the great day.*

Jude 7: *Even as Sodom and Gomorrha*, and the cities about them, in like manner, giving themselves over to fornication [i.e. homosexuality, sex perversions according to Matthew 5:23, Romans 1:24-32] and going after strange flesh, *are set forth as an example*, suffering the vengeance of eternal fire.

Hebrews 6:7-9: For the earth which drinketh the rain that cometh oft upon it, and bringeth forth herbs meet for them by whom it is dressed, receiveth blessings from God but *that which beareth thorns and briers is rejected, and is nigh unto cursing; whose end is to be burned.* But, beloved, we are persuaded better things of you, and things that accompany salvation, though we thus speak.

## ONE UNPARDONABLE SIN

**There is only one unpardonable sin, according to Matthew 12:32**: And whosoever speaketh a word against the Son of man, it shall be forgiven him: but whosoever speaketh against the Holy Ghost, it shall not be forgiven him, neither in this world, neither in the world to come.

**There is only one unpardonable sin, according to Mark 3:29**: But he that blaspheme against the Holy Ghost hath never forgiveness, but is in danger of eternal damnation [v. 30: because they said, He hath an unclean spirit.]

**There is only one unpardonable sin, according to Luke 12:10**: "and whosoever shall speak a word against the Son of man, it shall be forgiven him: but unto him that blaspheme against the Holy Ghost it shall not be forgiven."

**Promise to Rebels**: Jesus exposed the people who lied to him before the people: Matthew 22:18-19: But Jesus perceived their wickedness, and said, "Why tempt ye me, ye hypocrite?"

It is the longing of Almighty God that all shall be saved and know the glory of Almighty God. (See John 3:16, 1 Timothy 2:4; 2 Peter 3:9.) All are welcome and invited to come and partake of the water of life freely.

Acts 3:23: And it shall come to pass, that *every soul, which will not hear the prophet, shall be destroyed* from among the people.

Man is a free moral agent. If not, He (God) would be entirely responsible for all sin on the human race. It is impossible to serve God and Satan at the same time. (See Matthew 6:24; John 8:32-36; Romans 6:16-23; Revelation 8:12-13.)

God gave Pharaoh, the ruler of Egypt ten chances to let His people Israel go. When the King refused each time, God sent ten separate plagues over the course of nine months. Beginning in Exodus 7:14 and ending in

Exodus 12:30.

1.  The water was contaminated. (Note that the water in major cities in America are becoming contaminated.)
2.  Pestilences overran the land (i.e. rats, mice, and vermin)
3.  People and animals infected (i.e. AIDS.)
4.  Flies covered the land (i.e. more infection.)
5.  Disease killed the livestock (i.e. mad-cow disease.)
6.  Boils and sores infected people and their animals (i.e. Cancer.)
7.  Hail destruction of crops (Note that due to hail, tornadoes, drought and other factors, many of our farms are gone.)
8.  Swarms of locust covered the land and ruined crops (Note that every 7 yrs. we get these locusts)
9.  Darkness covered Egypt for three days.
10. The firstborn children and livestock were destroyed. (This is a picture of abortion.)

Just as He did with Pharaoh, God comes to us, time and time again.

*How many chances have you been given?*

*How many times have you turned your back on God?*

## FREE WILL TO CHOOSE

***Promises are given to man upon the bases of their choices:*** Matthew 16:24-25 says, "If any man will come after Me, let him deny himself, and take up his cross, and follow Me. For whosoever will save his life, shall lose it: and whosoever shall lose his life for My sake, shall find it." Refer to chapter 3 in the section about the 'Romans Road.' When you truly submit yourself to the Lord and are filled with the Holy Ghost, You realize He is with you, He is in you, and will be upon you as you serve Him.

My prayer for you is that your hunger can never be filled, nor your thirst quenched. Always long for more of Him, never be completely satisfied with what you have. ***There is so much more***. The more you long for him, the more He will give of Himself. Power is in the name of Jesus through faith, for this is the secret of power with God and all divine miracles.

Hebrews 13:5 He said, "I will never leave thee nor forsake thee." So that we may boldly say, "The Lord is my helper, and I will not fear what man shall do unto me."

*There is no other relationship on earth that we will ever experience that can compare to the friendship and the love of God, for He is faithful to keep all of His Promises made to us, in and through His Word!*
*Amen*

# ABOUT THE AUTHOR

Sheila Kay is an ordained and licensed minister under Gospel Crusades Fellowship in Stephens, Pennsylvania, and Cross Country World Missions in Rocky Mount, North Carolina. She is an ordained Stephens Minister and Trainer and has also ministered extensively in the prison system. Her ministry, *House of Prayer, Prophecy, and Healing,* in addition to her inner-city street ministry, *Restoring the Broken Vessel,* has blossomed into seven churches in the Maryland and Washington D.C. areas. Sheila is the daughter of a Jewish father and works with the Aliyah Return Center in Tiberias, Israel. She heads a monthly Prophetic Roundtable and has authored two books, *Maturing in Son-ship through Suffering* and *Promises: God's Provision through His Promises*. Sheila is a Certified Dietary Manager and Natural Health Consultant who teaches Certified Professional Food Service classes throughout the United States. Last but not least, Sheila is joyfully a great-grandmother.

# ABOUT MANIFEST PUBLICATIONS

Manifest Publications is the publishing division of Manifest International, LLC. Our objective is to help like-minded ministries and writers produce and distribute materials which proclaim the Gospel of Jesus Christ to all the world and equip the global Church for unity and maturity.

MANIFEST
PUBLICATIONS

www.manifestinternational.com

www.manifestbookstore.com